Editor: PENNY CLARKE
Artists: MARK BERGIN
JOHN JAMES
MARK PEPPÉ

Produced by
THE SALARIYA BOOK CO. LTD
25 Marlborough Place
Brighton BN1 1UB

Published in 1997 by
Macdonald Young Books
61 Western Road
Hove BN3 1JD

ISBN 0-7500-1917-4

Printed in Hong Kong.

A CIP catalogue record for this book is
available from the British Library.

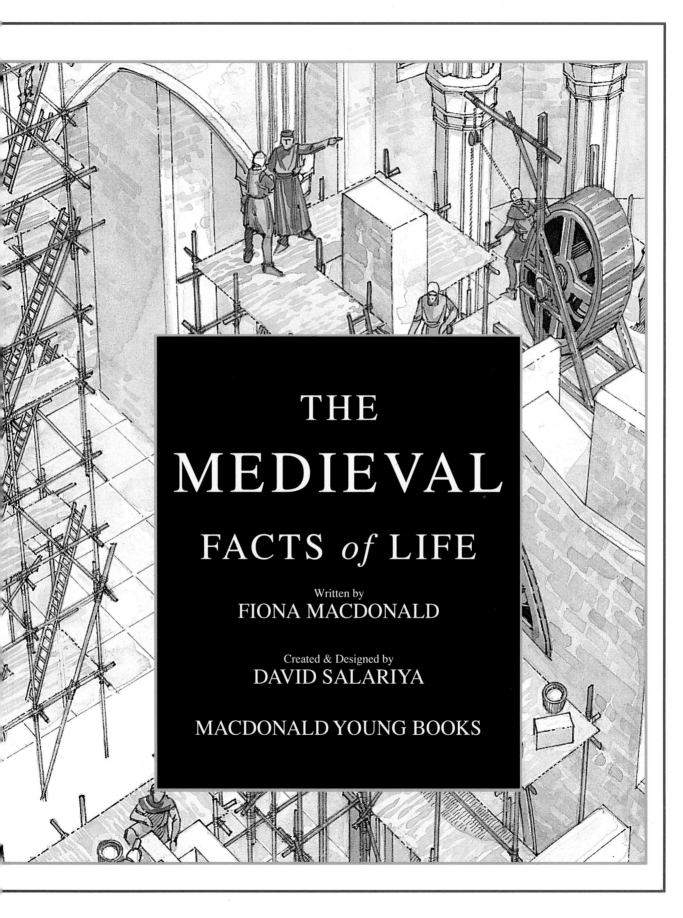

THE
MEDIEVAL
FACTS *of* LIFE

Written by
FIONA MACDONALD

Created & Designed by
DAVID SALARIYA

MACDONALD YOUNG BOOKS

Contents

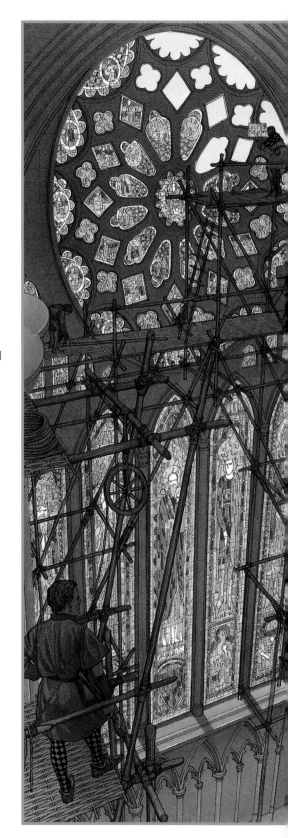

INTRODUCTION

THE PERIOD we call the Middle Ages (the years from AD 1000 to 1500) was a time of great contrasts – between mighty lords and powerless peasants, saintly bishops and bloodthirsty soldiers, scholarly nuns and kings who could not read. Differences between people of title, rank and status, mattered far more than today. Most men and women had little chance of moving out of the social group into which they had been born.

The Middle Ages was a time of great achievements in art, architecture, music, poetry and many highly skilled crafts. It was a time of great activity, when peasant farmers cut down virgin forests to clear new fields to grow food for their families, and experimented with better ways of growing crops. It was a time of violence and lawlessness, but also a time when many men and women devoted their lives and their fortunes to the Christian faith.

However, the Middle Ages was also a time with many problems. From the windows of their fine houses rich city merchants could see miserable beggars huddling at their gates. Magnificent castles, exquisite palaces and lofty cathedrals were built within a stone's throw of flimsy countryside hovels and stinking inner-city slums. Beautiful silk and velvet robes, embroidered with gold, might be crawling with lice and fleas. And, after the Black Death reached Europe in 1348, whole families could be wiped out by the plague within 24 hours.

FACT: KINGS CLAIMED THEIR POWER CAME FROM GOD

NOBLES were very rich and owned lots of land. They helped the king fight and gave him advice. Sometimes they rebelled, overthrew their king and put a new one on the throne.

LAWYERS and scribes (left) worked as government officials and also ran the law-courts. Priests (right) cared for people's souls. Senior priests acted as royal councillors.

WHEN MEDIEVAL KINGS were crowned, they were anointed with holy oil. This was said to show that God had chosen them to rule and that their body was sacred too. Attacking them would be like attacking God, a serious crime. Although most medieval kings claimed their power came from God, few ruled in a god-like way. Some were lazy, some were weak, others neglected their kingdoms or ruled harshly.

It was hard to be a successful king. You had to be a brave soldier, appoint the royal council (from nobles and church leaders), negotiate with Parliament, organize the civil service, make alliances with other rulers, and keep your subjects happy. You were responsible for taxes, the army and navy, and making new laws.

Facts about Medieval Life:

Rich noble people formed between 5% and 10% of the population. Another 5% were wealthy professionals – such as lawyers and merchants. Compared with them, the remaining 80% were poor.

There were no state welfare benefits in medieval times. If people fell ill, or could not find work, they had to rely on family or friends for help.

FOOT-SOLDIERS (left) were recruited from villages and towns. Knights (right) came from rich families and led their own parts of the army.

COUNTRY PEOPLE, called peasants, grew crops, raised animals and spun wool. In towns, ordinary people worked as traders and at various crafts.

KINGS AND LORDS built strong castles to protect their lands. In wartime all the local people took refuge inside the nearest castle, while nobles, knights and foot-soldiers fought off the enemy. A siege could last for months or even years.

FACT: CASTLES WERE EMPTY MOST OF THE TIME

TODAY, many impressive ruins of medieval castles remain throughout Europe, reminders of the wars fought in that period. Castles were built for defence. The earliest were simple wooden forts, hurriedly constructed to house a lord and his army in newly conquered lands. Later these first castles were rebuilt in stone, and became a safe place where the lord, his family and everyone working for him could shelter if they were attacked. By the end of the Middle Ages castles had become little more than status-symbols.

Building a castle could take years. Often, the person who commissioned it did not live to see it completed. It was also expensive. Even kings sometimes had to stop the work on their castles as they ran out of money.

workshops

CASTLE BUILDERS chose sites that would be easy to defend: steep cliffs, river banks and rocky coasts. For extra security the castle's keep, the central tower, was ringed with stone walls.

guardroom

ramparts

arrow slits

strong stone walls

Facts about Medieval Castles:

Castle servants often slept in the same room as their master and mistress to guard them.

Sometimes prisoners in castles were left to starve. One type of French prison was called an 'oubliette' – a 'place of forgetting'.

Castles were designed by engineers, but built by unskilled labourers. Edward I of England forced local peasants and prisoners to help on his castle building sites.

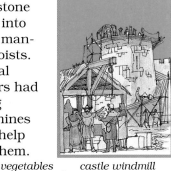

BLOCKS of stone were lifted into place with man-powered hoists. Medieval builders had no big machines to help them.

vegetables

castle windmill

cookhouse

THE GREAT HALL was the centre of castle life. There the lord and lady received visitors and entertained them with splendid feasts.

LAVATORIES were built within the thickness of the castle walls. Waste went down a chute to the castle moat below.

THE CASTLE's best bedroom was for the lord and his family. It was furnished with tapestries, carved wooden chests and a four-poster bed. The bed's curtains gave privacy and protection from draughts. Senior castle staff and guests had smaller rooms.

CASTLES had huge storerooms which were used to store fuel and food in case the castle was besieged.

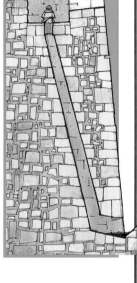

KINGS AND LORDS visited castles in wild forests to hunt deer and boar. Hunting and hawking were favourite medieval sports.

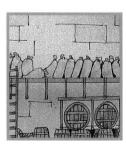

PRISONERS languished in damp dungeons, deep under-ground, which were infested with rats, lice and fleas.

WOMEN servants spun thread and wove woollen cloth.

11

FACT: PEASANTS WERE SMELLY

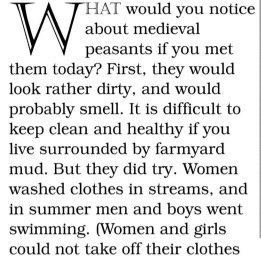

WHAT would you notice about medieval peasants if you met them today? First, they would look rather dirty, and would probably smell. It is difficult to keep clean and healthy if you live surrounded by farmyard mud. But they did try. Women washed clothes in streams, and in summer men and boys went swimming. (Women and girls could not take off their clothes in public.) Chewing twigs and rubbing salt into their gums was the only way they had to clean their teeth.

Second, you might think the peasants looked very old for their years. Hard work, hot sun and winter winds made hands knarled and skins rough and cracked. Accidents and diseases left painful limbs and, often, unsightly scars.

Third, the peasants would probably be unfriendly or even hostile. It was every villager's duty to be on the lookout for strangers, and to raise the alarm if they saw anyone suspicious.

BIG FARMS were very busy places, where many people lived. As well as the farmer, his family and their servants, there were ploughmen, shepherds, dairy-maids, cowherds, grooms and stable-lads.

FEBRUARY. Hard at work in the woods felling timber to use for building and making tools.

MARCH. Time to prune (cut back) the grape vines to encourage them to produce lots of grapes later in the year.

APRIL. Husband and wife dig their cottage garden. They grow garlic, cabbage and leeks to feed their family.

MAY. Bees are collecting nectar for honey from spring flowers. Medieval people used honey to sweeten food.

JUNE. Everyone helps cut the long grass in the meadows. It is dried as hay for winter feed for the animals.

JULY. The wheat is ripe and ready to harvest. It is cut with sickles (curved knives) and carted to the barn for storage.

Facts about Peasant Life:

During the 14th and 15th centuries, peasants revolted in many parts of Europe. They wanted to live and work where they chose, and refused to pay rents and taxes demanded by their lords in return for letting the peasants farm plots of their land.

We cannnot be certain (no one kept records then), but probably almost half the babies born to peasant families died in childhood of disease, accidents and malnourishment.

WATER for people and animals came from a deep well. It was hauled up in a leather bucket on a long chain.

PEASANTS took farm produce to the weekly market in the nearest town. They met friends and bought town-made goods.

AUGUST. Farm-workers use flails (heavy, jointed sticks) to separate the grains of wheat from the stalks.

SEPTEMBER. Ripe grapes are picked and trampled underfoot. The juice from the grapes is used to make wine.

OCTOBER. Time to plough and sow seeds of wheat, oats and barley. Without these crops, people will starve.

NOVEMBER. Pigs are taken to the woods to eat the fallen acorns and beechmast (nuts). They grow fat on this food.

DECEMBER. The fattened pigs are killed, the meat salted and hung over the smoky fire to make bacon and ham.

FACT: HOMES WERE MADE OF MUD AND WOOD

TODAY, many people think that medieval cottages look pretty and quaint. But what were they like to live in? In summer, they were probably cool and airy, thanks to the thick thatched roofs and unglazed windows, though the earth floors would have been dusty. In winter, most cottages would have been cold, damp and very draughty. The wattle-and-daub walls were thin, and wind whistled through the wooden shutters covering the windows.

These houses needed constant repairs. Timber frames rotted where they rested on the damp ground, plaster walls cracked, and birds, rats and mice nested in the roofs.

Families tried to warm their homes with fires, straw mattresses and thick blankets. But the fire filled the house with smoke, the straw was prickly and the blankets were rough.

ONLY well-off citizens could afford homes like these, with solid timber frames and rooms on two floors. Even so their furniture was simple: plain wooden tables and storage chests, benches for sitting and a feather mattress. The spinning wheel was a new invention in medieval times. The clay roof tiles helped to stop fires spreading in the crowded towns.

Facts about Medieval Homes:

In some parts of Europe peasants and their animals lived together in the same building. Body-heat from cows and horses gave extra warmth in winter, but in summer they would have been very smelly, and would have attracted lots of flies.

House-building techniques and styles varied, depending on the materials available. In regions with few trees, homes were built of mud bricks or stone.

IN THE COUNTRYSIDE peasants lived in simple, single-storey homes. The largest buildings in the village were the church, the windmill and the manor house. They usually all belonged to the local lord. He visited the manor house from time to time.

FACT: IT TOOK SEVEN YEARS TO LEARN A TRADE

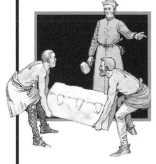

STONE-WORKERS
who were skilled
at detailed,
delicate work
trained as
sculptors.

ARCHITECTS
designed fine
buildings like
castles and
cathedrals.

MASONS used
heavy mallets
and chisels to
cut stone blocks
into shape.

APPRENTICES and
journeymen
mixed sand, lime
and water to
make mortar.

IN THE MIDDLE AGES almost every-
thing, from delicate jewellery to lumbering
farm carts, was made by hand. Medieval
craftsmen and women were highly skilled.

Crafts took many years to learn. Boys (and a
few girls) became apprentices when they were
7 or 8 years old. They went to live with a
master-craftsman and his wife. The craftsman
agreed to teach them his skills, to feed and
clothe them. In return, the apprentices helped
in the craftsman's workshop. After about seven
years, apprentices became 'journeymen' – fully
trained workers. Later, they might make a
masterpiece to qualify as a master. Then they
could open their own workshops.

BLACKSMITHS
made and
repaired iron
objects, like tools
and cooking-pots.
Specially skilled
metalworkers
might become
locksmiths.

CARPENTERS
(right) making
a wooden
frame to prop
up a partly
finished
arch.

A FEW MEN AND WOMEN made
a living as artists (left).
They painted holy pictures
on church walls and
portraits, too.

GLAZIERS made stained
glass windows by joining
small pieces of coloured
glass with lead strips to
make the design – usually
a biblical scene.

Towns needed strong walls and well-guarded gates to keep attackers out. Inside the walls there was always building work going on. Only the best built houses lasted more than 50 years.

The richest towns were usually centres of international trade, with a busy seaport or riverside quay.

Ships were the best way to carry heavy loads. Water transport was slow, but easier and safer than by land.

Medieval merchant ships were built with deep, rounded hulls to provide plenty of space for cargo.

Facts about Crafts:

Medieval towns were very small. Most had populations of less than 1000. But even so, you could find many crafts and trades, from weavers and dyers to candle-makers, tailors and goldsmiths.

Often there was little space inside the town's walls for new houses, so town houses were built several storeys high. Many of the houses had shops, warehouses and work-rooms on the ground floor.

FACT: POOR PEOPLE ATE THE PLATES OF THE RICH

IN MEDIEVAL TIMES what you ate depended on who you were. Peasants ate coarse brown bread, pea soup, cabbages, onions and garlic. If they were lucky, they might also have some ham or bacon, apples, pears and home-made cheese.

Nobles liked rich meat cooked in sauces with strong tastes. Medieval cookery books give recipes for hot and spicy dishes, flavoured with ginger and saffron, for sweet and sour foods, cooked with honey and unripe grapes, and for puddings made with eggs, almonds and cream. This was an unhealthy diet – nobles did not eat much fresh fruit (they thought it was harmful), bread or vegetables. In fact, they used trenchers, thick slices of bread, rather like disposable plates. They were used to soak up grease and spills, then given to the poor to eat.

A CAREFULLY packed cauldron (cooking-pot) could be used to cook several different foods at once over an open fire.

A BIG MEDIEVAL castle needed a big kitchen, too. The cooks might have to provide meals for a hundred people every day while the lord and his soldiers were staying there.

WHEAT from the lord's farms was ground into flour at the mill, then baked in the castle oven. Vegetables came from the castle garden.

Facts about Food in the Middle Ages:
Laws protected consumers from bad food. Bakers caught selling mouldy loaves were dragged through the streets tied to the back of a cart. Brewers whose ale was too weak were fined. Officials called ale-tasters tested the brew by sitting in it. If they stuck to the seat, the ale was strong and sweet enough.

Ale was an important drink because milk and cold water were unsafe. Cows might be diseased and water was often polluted by sewage.

MANY servants were needed to cook and serve dinner to the lord and his guests. Some are shown at the bottom of the page. After the meal, jesters and minstrels often entertained the diners.

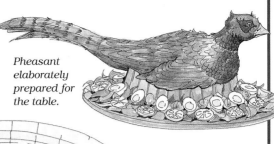

Pheasant elaborately prepared for the table.

MEDIEVAL people ate with their fingers, or with spoons and knives. Forks were not used.

DISHES for feasts could surprise – whole birds were baked in pies.

MEALTIME STAFF
1 Steward
2 Taster (checks for poison)
3 Pantler (keeps food stores)
4 Butler (keeps stores of drink)
5 Launderer (supplies clean table-cloths)
6 Cooks
7 Scullion (kitchen-boy)
8 Carver
9 Cup-bearer.

19

FACT: KNIGHTS AND SQUIRES WORE TIGHTS

THE RICH loved fine clothes – the finer the better. People in cities and nobles at court followed the latest fashions. By the 15th century these could be extreme: tall 'steeple' hats and low-cut dresses for young women; bottom-revealing tights and tunics and ridiculously pointed shoes for young men.

Older nobles, merchants, lawyers and their wives chose more sensible styles in expensive fabrics: silk, satin, velvet and fine wool. Craftsmen wore practical woollen tunics and hose with a linen shirt. Their wives wore woollen dresses and linen kerchiefs.

Peasants wore plain, simple clothes. In winter they wore several layers to try to keep warm.

HATS worn by fashionable men and women in the 14th century.

NOBLEWOMEN wore lavish styles like this fur-lined overtunic or pelisson.

Facts about Clothes:

Medieval people believed the smell from lavatories kept clothes-moths and their grubs (which eat fibres) away from woollen garments. So they hung their best robes there. Sometimes, 'garderobe' (wardrobe) was used as a polite word for lavatory.

The cost of a knight's clothes and armour would be like an expensive car today and his warhorse the equivalent of a small private jet.

OLDER MEN wore long robes, but young ones liked to wear tunics with tight-fitting leggings called hose.

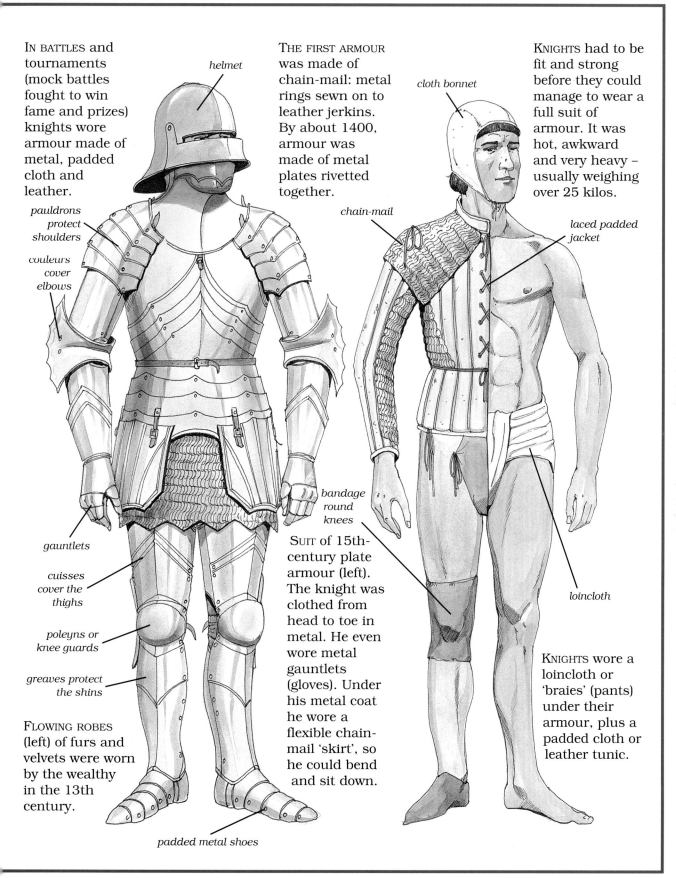

IN BATTLES and tournaments (mock battles fought to win fame and prizes) knights wore armour made of metal, padded cloth and leather.

helmet

pauldrons protect shoulders

couleurs cover elbows

gauntlets

cuisses cover the thighs

poleyns or knee guards

greaves protect the shins

FLOWING ROBES (left) of furs and velvets were worn by the wealthy in the 13th century.

padded metal shoes

THE FIRST ARMOUR was made of chain-mail: metal rings sewn on to leather jerkins. By about 1400, armour was made of metal plates rivetted together.

bandage round knees

SUIT of 15th-century plate armour (left). The knight was clothed from head to toe in metal. He even wore metal gauntlets (gloves). Under his metal coat he wore a flexible chain-mail 'skirt', so he could bend and sit down.

cloth bonnet

chain-mail

KNIGHTS had to be fit and strong before they could manage to wear a full suit of armour. It was hot, awkward and very heavy – usually weighing over 25 kilos.

laced padded jacket

loincloth

KNIGHTS wore a loincloth or 'braies' (pants) under their armour, plus a padded cloth or leather tunic.

FACT: MONKS AND NUNS SANG ALL NIGHT

ST BENEDICT (d.543), of the early Christian church, drew up rules to guide the lives of monks and nuns. He had divided the day into three: for work, prayer and sleep, but services, with hymns and chants, were to be held at intervals throughout the day and night.

Other religious people served God in different ways. Priests looked after the people in their parishes; friars travelled about, preaching. Their sermons often attracted vast crowds. Hermits and anchorites, solitary religious men and women, offered prayers, counselling and advice.

SOME MONASTERIES were attached to cathedrals, as at Durham, in the north of England (below). The monks there looked after the spiritual needs of pilgrims who visited the tomb of St Cuthbert, in the cathedral.

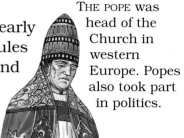
THE POPE was head of the Church in western Europe. Popes also took part in politics.

MOST VILLAGES had their own church – often paid for by the lord. Villagers were meant to attend services each Sunday, and on holy days, like Christmas.

Facts about Religous Life:
The village church was the setting for many important events in people's lives. Babies were baptized there, couples got married there, and the village's dead were buried in the churchyard.

Churchyards were also used for 'church ales', noisy, drunken community parties held to raise money for a good cause.

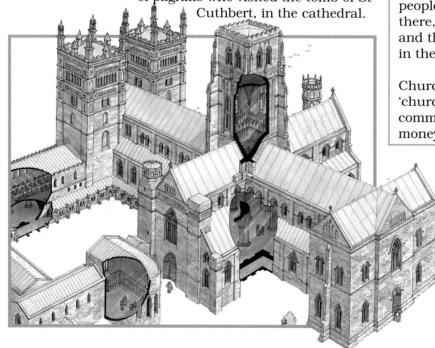

CATHEDRALS were usually built in city centres. They were large churches, where a bishop (a very senior priest) had his throne. All over Europe, bishops, city leaders, architects and builders tried to build the most beautiful cathedrals to glorify God and increase their city's prestige.

FACT: FIVE-YEAR OLDS COULD GET ENGAGED

IN THE EARLY Middle Ages, monasteries were the main centres of learning. But after around 1100, many schools and universities were built. They taught Latin, maths, music, philosophy, medicine and law.

MARRIAGE for love was rare. Among noble families marriages were arranged, often when children were still babies, to make political alliances, or to acquire land. Peasants were more likely to marry for love, but many peasant women married to find security and many peasant men to get a housekeeper, cleaner and cook.

Divorce was uncommon. The Church did not approve of it. But the rich could pay lawyers to persuade the Church to annul (cancel) a first marriage. An unhappy peasant just left his wife. Deserted women and children were among the poorest people in medieval society.

Facts about Marriage:

The average medieval marriage only lasted for about 15 years. Many women died in childbirth, and many young and middle-aged men were killed in battles or farm accidents. And diseases killed rich and poor, young and old, men and women.

For noblewomen marriage was a career, with many responsibilities. So young girls from rich or noble families were taught to read and write, to keep accounts, to manage servants, and to entertain important visitors with tact and charm.

Church law governed marriage. It taught that girls could marry when they were 12 years old and boys when they were 14.

CHILDREN from ordinary families did not go to school. Instead, they were trained by their parents at home. Boys were taught their father's occupation: farming, craftwork or a trade. Girls learned housework, gardening, nursing and babycare.

A BOY from a rich or noble household could train to be a knight. He lived in another noble's household from the age of eight. He learnt obedience, manners, riding, reading and writing.

LEARNING how to fight and use weapons was an important part of the training to become a knight.

MARRIAGE was a full-time job. A wife had to help her husband run his business, or manage his land while he was away.

MANY castles and manor houses had private rooms, called 'solars' where the lord and his family could relax peacefully together at the end of the day. They might listen to music or tell stories. Playing chess was another popular pastime.

FACT: HOLY DAYS BECAME HOLIDAYS

THERE were many oppportunities for medieval people to have fun. Church festivals and saints' days were holidays. They were celebrated with processions, music and dancing, with plays and puppet-shows, and with markets and fairs.

A pilgrimage was a different kind of religious holiday – a journey to a holy place, or a saint's shrine. Pilgrims hoped to win blessings, or forgiveness for their sins. But they knew they might not survive the pilgrimage. They made their wills before they left, for shipwreck or attacks by bandits were real dangers.

Medieval people enjoyed sports and games. Football was very popular. It was played with a pig's bladder for a ball, and sometimes became extremely violent. Often all the men in a village took part. Today we would probably consider other popular medieval sports, like bear-baiting and cock-fighting, very cruel.

NOT all entertainment was religious. Everyone enjoyed listening to minstrels or watching jugglers and acrobats.

A TOWERING cathedral spire and inns with soft beds and good food were welcome sights for pilgrims at the end of their long journey. A pilgrimage could be fun, but it might also be exhausting and dangerous.

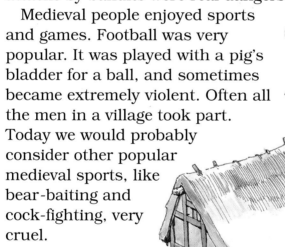

PILGRIMS took a shady hat, a roomy scrip (or shoulder bag), a warm cloak and a stick.

MANY great cathedrals had collections of saints' relics, which also attracted large crowds of pilgrims.

PILGRIMS lodged wherever they could – in barns or shepherds' huts, in farmhouses, or in special hostels (above) built beside popular pilgrim routes.

Facts about Holy Days:

A pilgrimage could take weeks, months or even years. Pilgrims on foot were unlikely to travel more than 20 kilometres a day, even along well-trodden pilgrim tracks.

Pilgrims liked to bring souvenirs home with them: flasks of holy water and metal badges which they pinned to their hats and cloaks.

RICH PILGRIMS travelled on horseback, but most ordinary people made pilgrimages on foot.

THE most popular pilgrimage places in medieval Europe were Rome (Italy), Canterbury (England) and Santiago de Compostela (Spain).

FACT: RATS AND FLEAS KILLED MILLIONS

MEDICAL TREATMENTS:
1 Removing a splinter
2 Setting a broken bone
3 Straightening a twisted elbow
4 Repositioning a dislocated shoulder
5 Nursing care
6 Blood-letting.

MEN AND WOMEN living in the Middle Ages faced far more pain and suffering than most people in Europe today. Doctors, apothecaries (chemists), nuns, midwives and wise women (witches) did their best with herbs, simple operations and nursing care, but they had few effective remedies. The Church taught that Christians should bear pain calmly. It might have been sent by God to purify the soul.

Medieval doctors were particularly helpless faced by bubonic plague, often called the 'Black Death'. The first signs of the disease were painful black swellings under the arms. Then came a burning fever and a purple rash all over the body. Few people recovered. The disease reached Europe from Asia in the 1340s, killing millions of people.

LEPROSY was much feared, and lepers had to ring bells to warn people away.

THERE were no anaesthetics, so patients having an operation were drugged with poisonous herbs or alcohol. Many died because germs infected their wounds.

SOME of the best hospitals were run by nuns. They believed it was their duty to care for the sick.

Medieval Medical Facts:

Medieval doctors believed some diseases were caused because the patient had too much blood. So they made cuts in their patients' veins to let the 'extra' blood drain away, or used leeches (water slugs) to suck it out.

Some medieval operations were extremely dangerous. For example, trepanning (cutting a hole in the skull) was meant to cure headaches. But it was more likely to kill the patient first.

Some people believed you would not catch the plague if you carried a lucky 'bezoar stone', or prayed to St Roche, or avoided alcoholic drink, rich food and sex. They were all proved wrong and most died.

Washing in vinegar was also believed to be a precaution. It was no more effective than the others.

MANY MEDIEVAL people lived in dirty, unhealthy conditions, without clean water, lavatories, or bathrooms. Monasteries (top) had underground drains and purpose-built lavatory blocks.

DOCTORS spent many years training. They charged so much for their treatments that only rich people could afford to go to them.

BODIES of plague victims were left in the streets, to be carted away for burial in mass graves, known as plague pits.

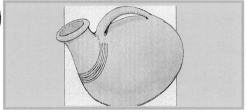

PLAGUE was spread by rat fleas. Whenever a flea bit someone, it injected deadly plague germs into their blood.

POTTERY URINE flask. Doctors examined urine to try to diagnose disease.

GLOSSARY

Anchorite Person dedicated to a religious life who lives alone.

Apprentices Children whose parents have made a formal agreement for them to learn craft skills in the home of a master-craftsman.

Beechmast Nuts of beech trees, once used to feed pigs.

Flails Heavy jointed sticks used to separate grains of wheat from the stalks. This process is called threshing.

Friar Member of a brotherhood of priests who travelled around preaching and teaching people the Christian faith.

Game A competitive sport; also wild animals and birds hunted for food or sport.

Hawking A popular medieval sport; specially trained birds of prey were used to hunt and kill small game birds and animals.

Hermit Man or woman who lives alone, devoting their time to God.

Jerkin Man's sleeveless jacket, often made of leather.

Journeyman Fully trained craftsman or woman who worked for a master-craftsman. (The term comes from journeé, the French for 'day'. Originally, journeymen hired themselves out to work for a day at a time.)

Kerchief Piece of cloth worn by women like a headscarf.

Leprosy Serious skin disease that eats away fingers and toes. Although feared by medieval people, it is now curable with drugs.

Masterpiece Extra fine piece of work made by a journeyman to prove he was good enough to become a master of his craft.

Mystery plays Plays on religious themes performed by craftsmen.

Relics The remains of saints. Medieval people believed they had supernatural powers.

Wattle-and-daub Medieval building material. Thin twigs were woven together and then coated with a mixture of mud or clay, horsehair and straw. Walls of wattle-and-daub were usually quite thin.